SWANS

LIVING WILD

Published by Creative Education

P.O. Box 227, Mankato, Minnesota 56002

Creative Education is an imprint of The Creative Company

Design and production by Mary Herrmann

Art direction by Rita Marshall

Printed in the United States of America

Photographs by Bridgeman Art Library (Walter Crane), Getty Images
(Jose Asel/Auora, Gareth Cattermole, Guy Edwards, Jeff Foott, Jonathan
Gale, Jo Hale, Leonardo da Vinci, Roine Magnusson, Eric Meola, Eastcott
Momatiuk, Michael S. Quinton, Norbert Rosing/National Geographic),
iStockphoto (Carlos Ameglio, Richard Bowden, Matthew Dixon, Grant
Dougall, cfsFinland, Manfred Konrad, Petr Mašek, Rich Phalin, Vladimirs
Prusakovs, Martin Sach, Sally Scott, Mikhail Soldatenkov, David Tyrer,
Tammy Wolfe)

Library of Congress Cataloging-in-Publication Data

Helget, Nicole.

Swans / by Nicole Helget.

p. cm. — (Living wild)

Includes index.

ISBN 978-1-58341-659-4

1. Swans—Juvenile literature. I. Title. II. Series.

QL696.A52H45 2008

598.4'18—dc22   2007015242

First Edition

9 8 7 6 5 4 3 2 1

✿ CREATIVE EDUCATION

SWANS

Nicole Helget

As gracefully as a ballerina

and as majestically as royalty,

the trumpeter swan

glides across the pond surface.

As gracefully as a ballerina and as majestically as royalty, the trumpeter swan glides across the pond surface. The setting summer sun casts a long shadow from the swan's body onto the rippling water. The stark white feathers of the swan seem to glow. Her long neck dips now and again into the water as delicately as a knife blade into the pulp of a melon. She pulls weeds from the depths with her black beak.

Soon, she returns to her nest along the shore, spreads her great wings, and flaps them dry. She settles atop her four white or tan eggs, her body heat causing the chicks inside the eggs to stir. Her partner swims toward the nest, too. He leans back his head and calls out to her. She stands and lifts her body up. She looks down at the eggs as if to tell them it's time to hatch.

WHERE IN THE WORLD THEY LIVE

■ **Tundra Swan**
also called whistling swan; northern coastlines of North America and northern Russia

☐ **Bewick's Swan**
northern coastlines of North America and northern Russia

☐ **Whooper Swan**
subarctic Eurasia, from northern Scandinavia to Siberia

■ **Mute Swan**
British Isles, north-central Europe, and north-central Asia

■ **Trumpeter Swan**
south-central Alaska, northwestern Canada, and midwestern United States

Swans can be found all around the world at different times of the year. These colored squares represent the seven species' primary breeding grounds, or where they live for most of the year until wintertime. During the winter, swans migrate to warmer areas, usually far south of their summer homes.

■ **Black-Necked Swan**
southern half of South America

■ **Black Swan**
throughout Australia

BEAUTIFUL, INSIDE AND OUT

Swans live on five of Earth's seven continents. Five of the seven swan species are white birds, large in stature and heavy in weight. These swans live in the Northern Hemisphere. The other two species are partially or fully black and somewhat smaller than their white counterparts. They live in the Southern Hemisphere.

The trumpeter swan is the largest of the swan species, weighing up to 40 pounds (18 kg), standing up to five feet tall (1.5 m), and spreading its wings nearly eight feet (2.4 m), from wingtip to wingtip. The trumpeter swan's scientific name is *Cygnus buccinator,* and it makes its home in northwestern and central North America. Swans are part of the Anatidae family. All members of this family are birds that have developed special **adaptations** for swimming, floating on the surface of water, and sometimes diving underwater to search for food. They have webbed feet, bills, and feathers that use special oils to shed water. Ducks and geese are also part of this family.

Another member of the Anatidae family, the tundra swan, is sometimes mistaken for a trumpeter swan. Close inspection reveals the differences, though. While the tundra swan's bill is concave and small in proportion to its head, the trumpeter swan's bill is heavy, wedge-shaped, and large in proportion to the rest of its body. The birds have markedly different calls as well. Tundra swans have high-pitched, quavering, "woo-woo" calls. Trumpeters have an unmistakably resonant, trumpet-like call.

The trumpeter swan has white **plumage** and a long neck. Its bill is black except for a pink stripe along its mouthline. The legs of the trumpeter are short and black. Trumpeter babies are gray in color for the first year, after which they turn white. All adult trumpeters experience a **molting** period in the summer, which involves losing some of their flight feathers. For female trumpeters, this period occurs shortly after their young hatch. They cannot fly at this time. The males molt about a month later.

Like a human's arm, a swan's wing is composed of the humerus bone, attached at the elbow to the radius and ulna bones. Swans also have a wrist that joins a three-fingered hand, which is covered with feathers. The wing bones of the swan are hollow so that they

Tundra swans (pictured) are similar in appearance to trumpeters, except for the yellow dot on the bill just under the eye.

If a swan's long flight feathers are clipped or damaged, they will eventually grow back, as human hair does.

don't add too much extra weight to the bird's body. This allows them to fly. A thin, strong skin grows over these bones and is covered by long flight feathers. The flight feathers are the wings that help the bird to fly. Eleven stiff flight feathers grow from the swan's wingtip. These feathers are narrow where they connect to the skin and then fan out. As a result, when the swan flaps its wings in flight, the feathers open like fingers, and more wind is forced through them.

Scientists think that birds were once closely related to reptiles and that feathers evolved from reptile scales as a way to help keep the animal warm in cooler climates or cold water. Feathers act as an **insulator** for trumpeter swans. They keep heat close to the swan's body and protect the skin from cold air. That is why trumpeter swans are able to live in cold climates. When a trumpeter flies south, its feathers protect its body from harmful sun rays, which could burn the swan's skin.

Feathers are also important in attracting a mate. A swan with a shabby feather coat will have a difficult time gaining the interest of another swan during the summer mating time. Clean and orderly feathers indicate health and vitality to other swans. Bald patches, unruly feathers, or dirty feathers indicate illness and old age to potential mates.

A swan has two inches (5 cm) of thick, fuzzy down feathers close to its skin. These feathers trap the warm air coming from the swan's body and keep it close to the swan's skin. A swan's feathers are so closely packed that it can withstand temperatures of –20 °F (–29 °C). On top of the downy feathers are a swan's flight and **contour feathers**. For up to six hours a day, as part of a process

John James Audubon was a famous American artist. He painted a picture of the trumpeter swan, along with many other North American birds, in 1838.

called preening, a swan uses its beak to pull the contour and flight feathers through its bill to press together the hook-like ends of the feather barbules.

Swans must keep their feathers in good condition to withstand the cold and the friction of flying. While preening, a swan secretes waterproof oil from the base of its tail. The oil is made of fat and wax. The swan applies this oil all over its more than 25,000 feathers to keep water out and to keep the feathers from drying out or fraying. Preening also moisturizes the bill and provides the swan with vitamins. Swans bathe and preen several times a day. Each preening takes about half an hour.

The trumpeter swan makes its home in the large, shallow ponds or the wide, slow rivers of the northern United States and central Canada. The breeding grounds of the trumpeter used to extend from the Bering Sea in the North Pacific Ocean east throughout most of Canada, and then south throughout Missouri, Illinois, and Indiana, but lax hunting laws prior to 1918 brought the bird close to complete extinction. Although trumpeter swans have battled back, their present-day population is nowhere near their former numbers.

A swan's preen gland, which secretes the fatty oil needed to waterproof its feathers, is located on the back near its tail.

A group of swans may be called a bevy, a flock, or a herd. A group of swans in flight is called a wedge.

Trumpeter swan flocks are now found from Alaska to Washington state, in the Great Basin region of Canada, in Yellowstone National Park, and in smaller flocks in western and midwestern states such as Oregon, Montana, Wyoming, South Dakota, and Minnesota. Wild trumpeters travel where the food is. They feed

on the vegetation found in rivers, lakes, and ponds, including the leaves, seeds, and roots of many types of pond weeds. Wild swans have also been spotted eating leftover grains and vegetables in fields that have been harvested by farmers. In captivity, swans will eat corn and other grains given to them.

Trumpeter swans will squawk loudly and flap their wings to fend off threats made to their nests.

MATES FOR LIFE

hen trumpeter swans reach two or three years of age, they pair up with a mate. Mates are usually chosen in the winter feeding grounds, even though the actual mating won't occur until the pair reaches their summer nesting grounds. In the winter feeding grounds, swans may get to know one another by bobbing their heads and facing one another. This courtship behavior continues after they fly north in the spring. In late March, the pair will construct a nest to prepare for their family. These mates will stay together throughout their lives, which may be as long as 20 years.

The male swan, called a cob, may try to clear the territory of all other waterfowl. He may squawk at and chase ducks and geese away from his nesting grounds. Ducks and geese, in particular, may try to take over the trumpeter swans' nest rather than build their own. The cob and his female mate, called a pen, usually choose a spot that is completely surrounded by water. This lessens the chance that land predators, such as foxes, will be able to reach the nest. Then the cob collects materials for the nest. He brings sticks, leaves, and reeds to the pen, and the pen assembles the nest.

Mute swans have gracefully curved necks.

Mute swans, found in Europe and western Asia, have 23 vertebrae in their necks, which is more than any other bird. Humans have only seven vertebrae.

A fox is an omnivore, which means it will eat whatever is available, be it grasses, berries, insects, mice, or swan eggs.

The process of building the nest, which can be between 6 and 11 feet (1.8–3.4 m) in diameter, takes the pair about two weeks. Building a large and sturdy nest is important because the trumpeter swan pair will use the same nest for three or four years. Even before the eggs are hatched, the pen will sit on the nest for long periods of time. She uses her body weight to compress the nest materials and make a cozy spot where she will be able to keep her eggs safe and warm.

The pen lays three to nine eggs at a time. A batch of eggs is called a clutch. Each egg is about four inches (10 cm) long and three inches (8 cm) wide. After the pen lays them, she'll spend most of her time sitting on the clutch to **incubate** and keep them safe from predators. Once in a while, the pen leaves the clutch for a brief time to eat or preen. Before she does, she carefully covers the eggs with leaves or reeds and calls to the cob to come stand guard. Once she's gone, a predator such as a fox may try to attack, or ducks and geese may try to take over the nest. The cob will defend the nest and the eggs. When he is successful, the cob and pen later perform a "triumph display," in which they face each

other, quivering their wings and trumpeting loudly.

After 35 days, the baby swans hatch. They are called cygnets (*SIG-nits*). The cygnets are covered in gray down, which helps keep them warm and **camouflaged** in the nest. They have no flight feathers at first, so they can't fly. They have pink bills and weigh only half a pound (227 g) each. A few days after hatching, the mother and father trumpeter swans will take their brood on a feeding **excursion**. The parents will lead the babies to the water, where the cob uses his bill to stir up tiny particles of water weeds or bring insect larvae to the surface. The parents

Trumpeter swans incubate their clutches of creamy white eggs for more than a month, rarely straying from the nest.

will show the babies how to peck at the food and eat it. When the cygnets are about a month old, they begin to eat bigger pieces of plants. By the time they are three months old, the cygnets can eat the same foods as their parents: roots, stems, leaves, and seeds.

When predators such as foxes or weasels prowl nearby, the cob and pen call out to their young in warning. The cygnets will quickly retreat to the safety of the nest. The pen may sit on top of her cygnets or stand nearby. If a predator comes closer, she may flap her wings and stretch out her neck. She will try to make herself look as large as possible to scare away the predator and protect her young. Not until late summer will the cygnets be able to fly away from danger. But even after they can fly, they will not fly away from their family.

Trumpeter swans stay with their parents for a year, learning how to swim, how to fly, and where to search for the best food. If they don't stay with their parents for the entire year, they will not learn how to survive. Unlike some other animals, cygnets are not born with **instincts** that tell them when or where to fly when the weather turns too cold to live in their habitat. Scientists aren't

Two books of the Bible, Leviticus and Deuteronomy, prohibit the consumption of swan meat by humans because swans are "unclean birds."

Trumpeter swans are highly protective of their young (opposite).

sure why trumpeter swans must learn this behavior. They know only that a trumpeter swan's capacity for learning and remembering is great.

When winter comes and food is locked beneath the icy surfaces, swan parents lead their families south to warmer climates, where food is more abundant. Some trumpeters fly 1,000 miles (1,609 km) or more to reach their destinations. Once they arrive, the cob and pen will build a new nest or settle into one made the year before with their family. The young swans must learn everything else they need to know in this time because, after winter passes, around March or April, the trumpeter swan parents will lead the young swans back to their northern nest and begin to prepare for their next brood.

Even after flying the **migration** route down and back only one time, the young swans will remember the way. Many times, even if their parents have started a new brood, they will allow the younger swans to fly with them. But after a year, the parent-child relationship becomes much more relaxed. The parents are no longer solely responsible for feeding and protecting the young swans. The young swans must now do these things on their own.

SWAN SYMBOLS

P eople have long been fascinated by swans. Even though trumpeter swans are concentrated now in only a few areas of the world, particularly in the U.S. and Canada, relatives of this species have lived all over the world at one time or another. Their beauty and grace have captured the interest and imaginations of cultures throughout history. Swans are commonly portrayed in art, poetry, and mythology. For many years, people tried to claim the swans' beauty by trapping and killing them for their plumage. Recent laws have changed this. Now people work to repopulate areas with swans and help **preserve** their natural habitats.

The most famous story about a swan is the fable of the Ugly Duckling. In it, Danish storyteller Hans Christian Andersen chronicles the life of a mother duck and her chicks. When the chicks hatch, all but one are cute, yellow, and fuzzy. The other one is large, gangly, and gray. Because of his appearance, the ugly duckling is mistreated by everyone else. The ugly duckling is never unkind to anyone, though. Eventually, the little yellow chicks turn into ducks, but the ugly little cygnet turns

In 1970, author E. B. White wrote *The Trumpet of the Swan,* a book about a swan without a voice who learns to play the trumpet.

A prince falls in love with a swan princess in the ballet Swan Lake.

A "swan song" is a common term that refers to a person or animal's last great effort in word or deed before death.

into a graceful, beautiful swan. All the other animals realize their mistake and apologize to the swan. Rather than gloat or hold a grudge, the swan forgives. Andersen created the tale of the ugly duckling to teach a moral lesson—that inner beauty is more important than outer appearances.

Many cultures have swan tales that have been set to music. In some, the swan is a symbol of true love, because wild swans mate for life. In others, the white swan is a symbol of purity and beauty. Nineteenth-century German composer Richard Wagner wrote two operas in which swans play a role: *Lohengrin*, a story about a young knight whose boat is pulled by swans as he goes off to rescue a maiden; and *Parsifal*, in which a swan is recklessly shot with an arrow and dies, teaching its shooter remorse. In *The Swan of Tuonela*, Finnish composer Jean Sibelius recreates the story of a mystical swan swimming around Tuonela, the island of the dead. The hero of the epic is supposed to kill the sacred swan, but on the way, he is shot with a poisoned arrow and dies. In the ballet *Swan Lake* by Russian Pyotr Tchaikovsky, a sorcerer's evil spell turns a princess

Swan Lake *premiered in 1877 as* The Lake of the Swans, *performed by the dancers from the Ballet of the Moscow Imperial Bolshoi Theatre. It is still staged all over the world today.*

THE WILD SWANS AT COOLE

The trees are in their autumn beauty,
The woodland paths are dry,
Under the October twilight the water
Mirrors a still sky;
Upon the brimming water among the stones
Are nine and fifty swans.

The nineteenth Autumn has come upon me
Since I first made my count;
I saw, before I had well finished,
All suddenly mount
And scatter wheeling in great broken rings
Upon their clamorous wings.

I have looked upon those brilliant creatures,
And now my heart is sore.
All's changed since I, hearing at twilight,
The first time on this shore,
The bell-beat of their wings above my head,
Trod with a lighter tread.

Unwearied still, lover by lover,
They paddle in the cold,
Companionable streams or climb the air;
Their hearts have not grown old;
Passion or conquest, wander where they will,
Attend upon them still.

But now they drift on the still water
Mysterious, beautiful;
Among what rushes will they build,
By what lake's edge or pool
Delight men's eyes, when I awake some day
To find they have flown away?

William Butler Yeats (1865–1939)

into a swan by night. By day, she is still a woman. A prince falls in love with her anyway, and the two drown themselves in the lake to be together forever.

In Ireland, a legend is told about a stepmother who transformed her children into swans for 900 years. It is called "The Children of Lir." In the story, a king remarries after the death of the queen and brings a stepmother into the castle to raise his four children. The stepmother dislikes the children and is jealous of their love for each other and for their father. She turns them into swans and releases them into the wild. Like real swans, they remain faithful to each other and stay together for 900 years as swans. Eventually, the spell expires.

Poets, too, have looked to the swan for inspiration. Nicaraguan poet Ruben Darío used the swan as a symbol of artistic inspiration, purity, and love. He drew attention to swan imagery in **Western** culture, including the love story of Leda and the swan. Euripedes, an ancient Greek poet, was one of the first to chronicle the tale of how the god Zeus, in the form of a swan, and Leda, a **mortal**, created the famously beautiful Helen of Troy. William Butler Yeats's poem, called "Leda and the Swan,"

Many stories about swans involve magical spells, but real swans in the wild are naturally enchanting.

Leonardo da Vinci's Head of a Young Woman with Tousled Hair or, Leda *(15th century)*

Like Helen of Troy, the Greek god Apollo's birth involved swans. Apollo's parents were Zeus and Leto. Apollo was born on an island inhabited only by swans.

recounted the tale to a 20th-century audience, portraying Zeus's role in a negative light. Yeats also wrote "The Wild Swans at Coole," in which the narrator observes a flock of beautiful swans on the same body of water year after year and wonders for how many more years the swans will come to that same place.

Swan maiden folktales are quite common in many countries. Typically, the swan maiden is robbed of her powers and forced to marry a human man. "The Feathery Robe" is a Japanese tale written around A.D. 690 about a young man who finds a coat made of whooper swan feathers. (The whooper swan is a close relative of the trumpeter swan but lives on the northern shores of Japan.) Just as the man puts the coat on, a beautiful maiden emerges from the water and demands the return of her coat. The young man offers a trade—a dance in exchange for the coat. The maiden obliges. Then she puts on her coat and rises into the air, spinning and singing until she disappears into the heavens.

Music and literature aren't the only arenas in which the swan is honored. Many religions over the centuries have also revered swans. In Hinduism, for instance, the swan is often associated with the goddess Saraswati, **patron** of knowledge, speech, poetry, and music. The swan sits at her side in paintings symbolizing these virtues. Catholics celebrate the holiness of St. Hugh of Lincoln by associating him with a white swan. Legend tells Catholics that St. Hugh once befriended a swan and took good care of him. In return, the swan guarded him while he slept. In this way, the swan represents love and loyalty.

In America and Europe, swan feathers were considered so beautiful and desirable that people hunted the animals until the early 1900s in order to take the long feathers from their wings. The sturdy flight feathers were then sold as writing quills or hair decorations. Other feathers were sold to be made into makeup puffs or pillow and mattress stuffing. Hundreds of years of over-hunting eventually took its toll on swan populations worldwide, and only a few hundred trumpeter swans could be found in the wild by the 1940s. The cygnets of the dead adult swans were left all alone and with no guides to lead them to the rivers and seacoasts of the U.S., where they wintered.

Some trumpeter swans can survive the cold winters without migrating.

When swans come in for a
landing, they circle the lake
many times, gradually flying
lower and lower.

ON THE MOVE

T rumpeter swans make interesting subjects for scientists hoping to uncover the mysteries of learned migration patterns. Today, researchers are conducting studies to determine whether or not young swans can be taught to migrate by humans rather than by adult swans.

When the first settlers came to the U.S. in the 1600s, 100,000 trumpeter swans wintered on the Atlantic coast. As more and more settlers came, they moved into the swans' breeding grounds. They shot the swans, pulled their feathers, and ate their meat. In 1769, the Hudson's Bay Company began selling swan skins and feathers to wealthy people for use as hat ornaments, clothing, and quills for writing. Swans were disappearing so rapidly that in 1912, one American **ornithologist** wrote, "The swan's total extinction is now only a matter of years." Indeed, only a few years later, no swans could be found east of the Mississippi River. People thought they had been lost completely.

Both the U.S. and Canada passed the Migratory Bird Treaty of 1918, which protected swans from hunters. In 1919, two trumpeter swan families were found in Yellow-

A group of swans in the wild is known as a herd, but a group of swans in captivity is referred to as a fleet.

stone National Park. Somehow, a small population had survived in the remote mountain valleys of Montana, Idaho, and Wyoming. The birds lived in relative seclusion and did not migrate, probably because the adult swans that knew how to migrate had been killed before they could pass on their knowledge. Safe from hunters, the trumpeters in Yellowstone increased their numbers to nearly 70 birds by 1932. Then, in 1955, a biologist reported finding a trumpeter swan breeding ground in Alaska.

But still, the trumpeter swans had a hard time increasing their populations because they stayed in the cold climates year-round and were more susceptible to illness and predators. In 1957, biologists began **transplanting** some of the swans into other areas of the U.S., including New York and Minnesota. The trumpeter swans reproduced at a satisfactory rate in those places but did not survive as well as they could have, had they known how to migrate.

Biologists were pleased with the swans' revival in the West, but they wanted the trumpeters to return to more of the eastern U.S., too. Established in the early 1980s, Trumpeter Swan Migration Projects in several states aimed to accomplish this goal. In New York, trumpeter

eggs were collected from captive nests and placed in automated incubators at the research facility. During incubation, biologists played an audiotape of a small engine. Even through the shell, cygnets learn to recognize their parents' voices. Since the biologists hoped to teach the cygnets to migrate by leading them with a small airplane called a "trike," they had to first make the engine

Even as adolescents, cygnets continue to learn behaviors, such as how to feed, from their parents.

Unlike mute and black swans, trumpeters do not tuck one foot behind the other when standing.

noise familiar to the baby birds. When the eggs hatched, the first thing they heard was the trike engine. The first things they saw were the biologists. As far as the cygnets were concerned, the biologists were their parents.

When the cygnets were just a few days old, the biologists began leading them around with the trike as it taxied on the ground. The biologists practiced with the birds for five months until their young muscles were strong enough to fly the 320-mile (514 km) migration route from northern New York to Chesapeake Bay, Maryland. Each swan was marked with a yellow band, indicating its participation in the special project. When the time came for the researchers to fly the swans south, the little swans flapped their wings and followed the plane. With a year of practice, the swans learned the route and were soon able to fly from their breeding to their wintering grounds on their own. Then, when the swans paired and mated, they were able to teach their cygnets the migration route.

Today, the study continues with new cygnets. Scientists hope that in a few years, the trumpeter swan population will be healthy enough for them to migrate on their own. Until then, studies like the one in New York and

Swan meat was considered a delicacy in medieval Europe. A medieval recipe for roasted swan calls for its blood to be used as food coloring.

other habitat conservation projects in Minnesota, Michigan, Iowa, and Canada are important. Threats to the restoration of the trumpeter swans include attacks from predators. One ironic result of protecting wildlife habitats is that predators as well as prey benefit. Mink, snapping turtles, great horned owls, coyotes, and red fox populations have increased in the same areas as the trumpeter swans. All of these predators will prey on cygnets if given the opportunity.

Far greater threats are illegal hunting or accidental shootings by humans. Trumpeter swans look a little like snow geese, which are legal to hunt. Sometimes, hunters confuse the two and accidentally shoot a trumpeter swan rather than a snow goose. Department of Natural Resources (DNR) workers in the U.S. contend that reckless shooting of trumpeter swans is a far greater problem than accidental shootings, though. Therefore, the fine for killing a trumpeter swan is steep. Fines range from $1,500 to $17,000 per bird.

Lead poisoning from contaminated water is

Without a parent to teach it how to fly, a cygnet must learn by other means or never be able to migrate.

When swans feed on plants in the water, it is called "dabbling"—they do not dive as some ducks do.

another problem trumpeter swans face. Lead-based fishing sinkers, which pull the hook deep into the water, can poison trumpeter swans when they are ingested as the swan feeds. A nationwide ban on lead-based fishing equipment went into effect in the early 1990s, but cleaning up the remaining sinkers is difficult. The DNR now encourages fishermen to not use old sinkers.

Power lines also pose a problem for trumpeter swans. Over the years, more and more power lines have crossed the skies where trumpeter swans fly. The thin lines are hard for the swans to detect, and sometimes a swan will fly into one, becoming injured and eventually dying. After much study, people have discovered that attaching large, bright objects to the power lines enables swans to see and avoid them. That is why there are large orange balls attached to power lines near bodies of water.

Trumpeter swans bring grace and beauty to the areas in which they live. With the help of scientists' research and laws to protect their lives and habitats, the swans' futures are bright. With their populations on the rise, and forgotten migratory routes being reintroduced, trumpeter swans will soar through the skies for many years to come.

In late summer, high in the night sky, you can see the Cygnus constellation. The nine stars of Cygnus form the shape of a swan.

ANIMAL TALE: LEDA AND THE SWAN

An ancient Greek myth recounts the parentage of the beautiful Helen of Troy, who was the cause of the Trojan War between the Greek states of Troy and Sparta. Helen's beauty, it is said, came from the pairing of her mother, a beautiful mortal named Leda, and her father, Zeus, the king of the gods, who, according to Greek mythology, took the form of a swan.

A long time ago, a woman named Leda married a Spartan king. The king was very busy with political affairs and paid little attention to his wife. She grew lonely. She wanted to have children. Every day she sat at her bedroom window knitting baby blankets and clothing for children she hoped to have. She stared out at the busy city of Sparta and wished for a better life.

Zeus, the greatest of all the gods, looked down upon Leda and felt sorry for her. Zeus had many powers, one of which was the ability to change into the form of any living creature. One day, he turned himself into a swan, the most beautiful of all flying creatures, so that he could sail over the earth undetected.

Zeus soared over many lands. But just as he flew over Sparta, a giant eagle with sharp talons began chasing him. The eagle scratched a big scrape in Zeus's back, and Zeus tumbled from the sky and landed on the windowsill of Leda's bedroom. Leda put down her knitting and ran to the window. She opened it and saw the beautiful swan with the wounded back.

"Beautiful creature," she said. "What has happened to you?"

Zeus had the power to heal himself and to change back into a god. But he remembered Leda's unhappiness and wanted to test her kindness and determine whether or not she was worthy of being a mother. So he allowed her to help him.

Leda took the swan and laid it on top of the blankets she had knit. She warmed water and washed the wound on the swan's back. She lay with it all night to keep it safe and warm. Zeus, the swan, cuddled close to Leda and determined that she was a worthy woman.

That night, Leda's husband came home from war. The next morning, Zeus, still in the form of a swan, flew out of the window and up into the Spartan sky.

Several months later, Leda gave birth to four children. Two were born mortal, but the other two were immortal and hatched from swan eggs as a reminder of the swan. One of the children from the eggs was Helen, who became the most beautiful woman in all of Sparta. Helen grew up and married a Spartan prince but later fell in love with a Trojan prince and left Sparta to join him. The Spartan prince grew angry and sent a thousand war ships to Troy to retrieve her. The Trojan prince was killed in the war, forcing Helen to go home with her Spartan husband. He was so angry with Helen that he decided to kill her. But as he raised his sword to slay her, Helen tilted her face toward him. He was so taken by her beauty that he put down his sword and let her live.

GLOSSARY

adaptations – changes an animal makes to improve its condition in its environment

camouflaged – hidden, due to coloring or markings that blend in with a given environment

contour feathers – the outermost feathers of a bird; they follow the shape of the bird's body

excursion – a short trip with a special purpose

incubate – to sit upon eggs and keep them warm until they hatch

instincts – natural impulses

insulator – material that keeps warmth in and cold out

migration – swans' practice of flying to a warmer climate

molting – the periodic shedding of all or part of an outer covering such as feathers

mortal – a creature or human who is capable of dying

ornithologist – a scientist who specializes in the study of birds

patron – one that supports a cause or protects those associated with a cause

plumage – the entire feathery covering of a bird

preserve – to keep alive or in existence

transplanting – moving from one place to another

Western – of or originating from the West, as in Europe or the U.S.

SELECTED BIBLIOGRAPHY

Cooper, Jason. *Trumpeter Swans: Giants among Us*. Vero Beach, Fla.: Rourke Publishing, 1997.

Featherly, Jay. *Ko-Hoh, The Call of the Trumpeter Swan*. Minneapolis, Minn.: Lerner Publishing Group, 1986.

Hansen, Skylar. *The Trumpeter Swan, A White Perfection*. Flagstaff, Ariz.: Northland Press, 1984.

Osbourne, Elinor. *Project Ultraswan*. New York: Houghton Mifflin, 2002.

U.S. Department of the Interior, U.S. Department of Fish and Wildlife. "Trumpeter Swan." Wildlife Biologue. http://training.fws.gov/library/Pubs/swan.pdf.

White, E. B. *The Trumpet of the Swan*. New York: HarperTrophy, 1970.

Only 8 to 10 weeks after their birth, cygnets are fully feathered and have reached half their adult size.

INDEX